THE VILLAGE COQUETTES. A COMIC OPERA. IN TWO ACTS

Libretto by Charles Dickens. Music by John Hullah

Charles Dickens (1812-1870) is regarded by many readers and literary critics to be THE major English novelist of the Victorian Age. He is remembered today as the author of a series of weighty novels which have been translated into many languages and promoted to the rank of World Classics. The latter include, but are not limited to, *The Adventures of Oliver Twist*, *A Tale of Two Cities*, *David Copperfield*, *A Christmas Carol*, *Hard Times*, *Great Expectations* and *The Old Curiosity Shop*.

His talents extended to many other forms including short stories, poetry, letters and his serial magazines. Of course being such a talent he also wrote plays. We are very pleased to present his second of four plays first performed at St. James's Theatre, December 6, 1836

Index Of Contents

DEDICATION

To J. P. HARLEY, ESQ.

MY DEAR SIR,

My dramatic bantlings are no sooner born, than you father them. You have made my 'Strange Gentleman' exclusively your own; you have adopted Martin Stokes with equal readiness; and you still profess your willingness to do the same kind office for all future scions of the same stock.

I dedicate to you the first play I ever published; and you made for the me the first play I ever produced:—the balance is in your favour, and I am afraid it will remain so.

That you may long contribute to the amusement of the public, and long be spared to shed a lustre, by the honour and integrity of your public life, on the profession which for many years you have done so much to uphold, is the sincere and earnest wish of, my dear Sir,

Yours most faithfully,

CHARLES DICKENS.

December 15th, 1836.

PREFACE

'Either the Honourable Gentleman is in the right, or he is not,' is a phrase in very common use within the walls of Parliament. This drama may have a plot, or it may not; and the songs may be poetry, or they may not; and the whole affair, from beginning to end, may be great nonsense, or it may not, just as the honourable gentleman or lady who reads it may happen to think. So, retaining his own private and particular opinion upon the subject (an opinion which he formed upwards of a year ago, when he wrote the piece), the Author leaves every such gentleman or lady, to form his or hers, as he or she may think proper, without saying one word to influence or conciliate them.

All he wishes to say is this; That he hopes MR. BRAHAM, and all the performers who assisted in the representation of this opera, will accept his warmest thanks for the interest they evinced in it, from its very first rehearsal, and for their zealous efforts in his behalf—efforts which have crowned it with a degree of success far exceeding his most sanguine anticipations; and of which no form of words could speak his acknowledgment.

It is needless to add that the libretto of an opera must be, to a certain extent, a mere vehicle for the music; and that it is scarcely fair or reasonable to judge it by those strict rules of criticism which would be justly applicable to a five-act tragedy, or a finished comedy.

DRAMATIS PERSONÆ

SQUIRE NORTON (Played by MR. BRAHAM).

THE HON. SPARKINS FLAM (his friend) (Played by MR. M. BARNETT).

OLD BENSON (a small farmer) (Played by MR. STRICKLAND).

MR. MARTIN STOKES (a very small farmer with a very large circle of particular friends) (Played by MR. HARLEY).

GEORGE EDMUNDS (betrothed to Lucy) (Played by MR. BENNETT).

YOUNG BENSON (Played by MR. J. PARRY).

JOHN MADDOX (attached to Rose) (Played by MR. GARDNER).

LUCY BENSON (Played by MISS RAINFORTH).

ROSE (her cousin) (Played by MISS J. SMITH).

PERIOD. THE AUTUMN of 1729.

SCENE. AN ENGLISH VILLAGE.

THE VILLAGE COQUETTES

ACT I

SCENE I.—A Rick-yard, with a cart laden with corn-sheaves. JOHN MADDOX, and labourers, unloading it. Implements of husbandry, etc., lie scattered about. A gate on one side. JOHN MADDOX is in the cart, and dismounts at the conclusion of the Chorus.

Round.
Hail to the merry Autumn days, when yellow cornfields shine,
Far brighter than the costly cup that holds the monarch's wine!
Hail to the merry harvest time, the gayest of the year,
The time of rich and bounteous crops, rejoicing, and good cheer!

'Tis pleasant on a fine Spring morn to see the buds expand,
'Tis pleasant in the Summer time to view the teeming land;
'Tis pleasant on a Winter's night to crouch around the blaze,—
But what are joys like these, my boys, to Autumn's merry days!

Then hail to merry Autumn days, when yellow corn-fields shine,
Far brighter than the costly cup that holds the monarch's wine!
And hail to merry harvest time, the gayest of the year,
The time of rich and bounteous crops, rejoicing, and good cheer!

JOHN. Well done, my lads; a good day's work, and a warm one. Here, Tom (to Villager), run into the house, and ask Miss Rose to send out some beer for the men, and a jug for Master Maddox; and d'ye hear, Tom, tell Miss Rose it's a fine evening, and that if she'll step out herself, it'll do her good, and do me good into the bargain. (Exit Villager.) That's right, my lads, stow these sheaves away, before the sun goes down. Let's begin fresh in the morning, without any leavings of to-day. By this time to-morrow the last load will have been carried, and then for our Harvest-Home!

VILLAGERS. Hurrah! Hurrah!

(First four lines of Round repeated.)

Enter MARTIN STOKES.

MARTIN. Very good! very good, indeed!—always sing while you work—capital custom! I always do when I work, and I never work at all when I can help it;—another capital custom. John, old fellow, how are you?—give us your hand,—hearty squeeze,—good shake,—capital custom number three. Fine dry weather for the harvest, John. Talking of that, I'm dry too: you always give away plenty of beer, here;—capital custom number four. Trouble you for the loan of that can, John.

JOHN (taking it from the cart). Here's the can, but as to there being anything good in it it's as dry as the weather, and as empty as you. Hoo! hoo! (laughing boisterously, is suddenly checked by a look from MARTIN).

MARTIN. Hallo, John, hallo! I have often told you before, Mr. Maddox, that I don't consider you in a situation of life which entitles you to make jokes, far less to laugh at 'em. If you must make a joke, do it solemnly, and respectfully. If I laugh, that's quite enough, and it must be far more gratifying to your feelings than any contortions of that enormous mouth of yours.

JOHN. Well, perhaps, as you say, I ought n't to make jokes till I arrive, like you, at the dignity of a small piece of ground and a cottage; but I must laugh at a joke, sometimes.

MARTIN. Must, must you!—Rather presuming fellow, this Maddox. (Aside.)

JOHN. Why, when you make one of them rum jokes of yours,—'cod, I must laugh then!

MARTIN. Oh! ah! you may laugh then, John; always laugh at my jokes,—capital custom number five; no harm in that, because you can't help it, you know.—Knowing fellow, though. (Aside.)

JOHN. Remember that joke about the old cow, as you made five years ago?—'cod, that was a joke! Hoo! hoo! hoo!—I never shall forget that joke. I never see a cow, to this day, without laughing.

MARTIN. Ha! ha! ha! very good, very good!—Devilish clever fellow this! (Aside.) Well, Jack, you behave yourself well, all the evening, and perhaps I may make that joke again before the day's out.

JOHN. Thank 'ee, that's very kind.

MARTIN. Don't mention it, don't mention it; but I say, John, I called to speak to you about more important matters.—Something wrong here, an't there? (Mysteriously.)

JOHN. Wrong! you're always fancying something wrong.

MARTIN. Fancying,—come, I like that. I say, why don't you keep your harvest-home at home, to-morrow night? Why are we all to go up to the Squire's, as if we couldn't be merry in Benson's barn? And why is the Squire always coming down here, looking after some people, and cutting out other people?—an't that wrong? Where's George Edmunds—old Benson's so fond of, and that Lucy was fond of too, once upon a time,—eh? An't that wrong? Where's your sweetheart, Rose?—An't her walkings, and gigglings, and whisperings, and simperings, with the Squire's friend, Mr. Sparkins Flam, the talk of the whole place? Nothing wrong there,—eh? (MADDOX goes up.) Had him there; I knew there was something wrong. I'll keep a sharp eye upon these doings, for I don't like these new-fangled customs. It was all very well in the old time, to see the Squire's father come riding among the people on his bay cob, nodding to the common folks, shaking hands with me, and all that sort of thing; but when you change the old country-gentleman into a dashing fop from London, and the steady old steward into Mr. Sparkins Flam, the case is very different. We shall see,—but if I might tell Miss Lucy Benson a bit of my mind, I should say, 'Stick to an independent young fellow, like George Edmunds, and depend upon it you will be happier than you would with all the show and glitter of a squire's lady.' And I should say to Rose, very solemn, 'Rose—'

ROSE enters unperceived, with beer.

'Rose—'

ROSE (starting). Lord bless us! What a hollow voice!—Why, it's Mr. Stokes!—What on earth is the matter with him?

MARTIN (not seeing her). Rose,—if you would be happy and contented, if you would escape destruction, shield yourself from dangerous peril, and save yourself from horrid ruin!—

ROSE. What dreadful words!—

MARTIN. You will at once, and without delay, bestow your hand on John Maddox; or if you would aspire to a higher rank in life, and a loftier station in society, you will cultivate the affections of Mr. Stokes,—Mr. Martin Stokes,—a young gentleman of great mental attractions, and very considerable personal charms; leaving the false and fatal Flam to the ignominious fate which—

ROSE. Why, Mr. Stokes.—

MARTIN. Ignominious fate which—

ROSE. Dear, he must be in a fit! Mr. Stokes!

MARTIN. Eh?—Ah! Miss Rose,—It's you, is it?

ROSE. Me! Yes, and here have I been waiting all this time, while you were talking nonsense to yourself. Here, I have brought you some beer.

MARTIN. Oh! Miss Rose, if you go on in this way, you'll bring us to our bier, instead of bringing our beer to us. (Looking round.) You may laugh, if you want to, very much, John.

JOHN. Hoo! hoo! hoo!

ROSE. Be quiet, oaf! And pray, sir (to MARTIN), to what may your most humorous observation refer?

MARTIN. Why, my dear Miss Rose, you know my way,—always friendly,—always thinking of the welfare of those I like best, and very seldom receiving any gratitude in return.

ROSE. I know you very seldom deserve any.

MARTIN. Ah! that's exactly my meaning; that's the way, you see. The moment I begin to throw out a hint to one of my dear friends, out comes some unkind and rude remark. But I bear it all for their sakes. I won't allow you to raise my ill nature,—you shan't stop me. I was going to say, don't you think—now don't you think—that you—don't be angry—make rather—don't colour up,—rather too free with Mr. Sparkins Flam?

ROSE. I make free with Mr. Sparkins Flam! Why you odious, insolent creature!

MARTIN. Ah, of course—always the way—I told you so—I knew you'd say that.

ROSE. And you, John, you mean-spirited scarecrow; will you stand there, and see me insulted by an officious, impertinent—

MARTIN. Go on, go on! (A gun fired.) Hallo! (Looking off.) Here they are, the Squire and Mr. Sparkins Flam.

ROSE (hastily adjusting her dress). My goodness! Mr. Spar—run, John, run, there's a dear!

JOHN (not moving). Very dear, I dare say.

ROSE. Run, and tell my uncle and Lucy, that Mr. Spar—I mean that the Squire's coming.

JOHN. I wouldn't ha' gone anyhow; but nobody need go now, for here they are. Now, I'm extinguished for the rest of the day.

Enter through the gate SQUIRE NORTON and MR. SPARKINS FLAM, dressed for sporting, with guns, etc., and two Gamekeepers. On the other side, old BENSON and LUCY. MARTIN, during the whole scene, thrusts himself in the SQUIRE'S way, to be taken notice of.

SQUIRE (to Gamekeeper, and putting down his gun). Take the birds into the house. Benson, we have had a good day's sport, but a tiring one; and as the load is heavy for my fellows, you'll let our game remain where it is. I could not offer it to a better friend.

BENSON. Your honour's very good, but—

SQUIRE. Nay, you make a merit of receiving the smallest favour.

BENSON. Not a merit of receiving, nor a boast of refusing it; but a man in humble station should be cautious how he receives favours from those above him, which he never asks, and can never return. I have had too many such favours forced upon me by your honour, lately, and would rather not increase the number.

SQUIRE. But such a trifle—

BENSON. A trifle from an equal, but a condescension from a superior. Let your men carry your birds up to the Hall, sir, or, if they are tired, mine shall do it for them, and welcome. (Retires up.)

FLAM (aside). Swine and independence! Leather breeches and liberty!

SQUIRE. At least I may be permitted to leave a few brace, as a present to the ladies. Lucy, I hope, will not object. (Crosses to her.)

LUCY. I feel much flattered by your honour's politeness—and—and—and—

ROSE. My cousin means to say, sir, that we're very much obliged to your honour and Mr. Flam for your politeness, and that we are very willing to accept of anything, your honour.

FLAM (aside). Condescending little savage!

SQUIRE. You have spoken very well, both for yourself and your cousin. Flam, this is Rose—the pretty little Rose, you know.

FLAM. Know! can I ever forget the charming Rose—the beautiful—the—the—(aside) the Cabbage Rose!

SQUIRE (aside). Keep that girl engaged, while I talk to the other one.

ROSE. Oh, Mr. Flam!

FLAM. Oh, Miss Rose! (He salutes her.)

BENSON. Your honour will not object to taste our ale, after your day's sport. The afternoon is fresh and cool, and 'twill be pleasant here in the air. Here, Ben, Thomas, bring mugs here—quick—quick—and a seat for his honour.

[Exeunt BENSON, MADDOX, etc.

SQUIRE. It will be delightful—won't it, Flam?

FLAM. Inexpressibly charming! (Aside.) An amateur tea-garden. (He retires a little up with ROSE—she coquetting.)

SQUIRE (to LUCY.) And in such society, how much the pleasure will be enhanced!

LUCY. Your honour knows I ought not to listen to you—George Edmunds would—

SQUIRE. Edmunds! a rustic!—you cannot love that Edmunds, Lucy. Forget him—remember your own worth.

LUCY. I wish I could, sir. My heart will tell me though, weak and silly as I am, that I cannot better show the consciousness of my own worth, than by remaining true to my first and early love. Your honour rouses my foolish pride; but real true love is not to be forgotten easily.

Song.—LUCY.

> Love is not a feeling to pass away,
> Like the balmy breath of a summer day;
> It is not—it cannot be—laid aside;
> It is not a thing to forget or hide.
> It clings to the heart, ah, woe is me!
> As the ivy clings to the old oak tree.
>
> Love is not a passion of earthly mould,
> As a thirst for honour, or fame, or gold:
> For when all these wishes have died away,
> The deep strong love of a brighter day,
> Though nourish'd in secret, consumes the more,
> As the slow rust eats to the iron's core.

Re-enter OLD BENSON, JOHN MADDOX, and Villagers, with jugs, seats, etc.; SQUIRE NORTON seats himself next LUCY, and ROSE contrives to sit next MR. SPARKINS FLAM, which MARTIN and MADDOX in vain endeavour to prevent.

SQUIRE. Flam, you know these honest people? all tenants of my own.

FLAM. Oh, yes, I know 'em—pleasant fellows!—This—this is—what's his name?

BENSON. Martin, sir,—Martin Stokes.

MARTIN (starting forward). A—a—Mr. Stokes at your service, sir,—how do you do, sir? (shaking FLAM by the hand, while speaking). I hope you are quite well, sir; I am delighted to see you looking so well, sir. I hope your majestic father, and your fashionable mother, are in the enjoyment of good health, sir. I should have spoken to you before, sir, only you have been so very much engaged, that I couldn't succeed in catching your honourable eye;—very happy to see you, sir.

FLAM. Ah. Pleasant fellow, this Martin!—agreeable manners,—no reserve about him.

MARTIN. Sir, you do me a great deal of honour. Mr. Norton, sir, I have the honour of drinking your remarkably good health,—I admire you, sir.

SQUIRE (laughing). Sir, I feel highly gratified, I'm sure.

MARTIN (aside). He's gratified!—I flatter myself I have produced a slight impression here. (Drinks.)

FLAM (turns round, sees MADDOX). Ah, Ox!

JOHN. Ox! Who do you call Ox? Maddox is my name.

FLAM. Oh, mad Ox! true; I forgot the lunacy:—your health, mad Ox.

SQUIRE (rising and coming forward). Come, Flam, another glass. Here, friends, is success to our Harvest-Home!

MARTIN. Hear, hear! a most appropriate toast, most eloquently given,—a charming sentiment, delightfully expressed. Gentlemen (to Villagers), allow me to have the pleasure of proposing Mr. Norton, if you please. Take your time from me. (He gives the time, and they all cheer.) Mr. Norton, sir, I beg to call upon you for a song.

Song.—SQUIRE NORTON.

> That very wise head, old Æsop, said,
> The bow should be sometimes loose;
>
> Keep it tight for ever, the string you sever:—
> Let's turn his old moral to use.
>
> The world forget, and let us yet,
> The glass our spirits buoying,

Revel to-night in those moments bright
Which make life worth enjoying.

The cares of the day, old moralists say,
Are quite enough to perplex one;

Then drive to-day's sorrow away till to-morrow,
And then put it off till the next one.

Chorus.—The cares of the day, etc.

Some plodding old crones, the heartless drones!
Appeal to my cool reflection,

And ask me whether such nights can ever
Charm sober recollection.

Yes, yes! I cry, I'll grieve and die,
When those I love forsake me;

But while friends so dear surround me here,
Let Care, if he can, o'ertake me.

Chorus.—The cares of the day, etc.

(During the Chorus, SQUIRE NORTON and FLAM resume their guns, and go up the stage, followed by the various characters. The Chorus concludes as the Scene closes.)

SCENE II.—An open spot near the village, with stile and pathway leading to the church, which is seen in the distance.

GEORGE EDMUNDS enters, with a stick in his hand.

EDMUNDS. How thickly the fallen leaves lie scattered at the feet of that old row of elm-trees! When I first met Lucy on this spot, it was a fine spring day, and those same leaves were trembling in the sunshine, as green and bright as if their beauty would last for ever. What a contrast they present now, and how true an emblem of my own lost happiness!

Song.—GEORGE EDMUNDS.

Autumn leaves, autumn leaves, lie strewn around me here;
Autumn leaves, autumn leaves, how sad, how cold, how drear!
    How like the hopes of childhood's day,
    Thick clustering on the bough!
    How like those hopes is their decay,—
    How faded are they now!

Autumn leaves, autumn leaves, lie strewn around me here;
Autumn leaves, autumn leaves, how sad, how cold, how drear!

Wither'd leaves, wither'd leaves, that fly before the gale;
Wither'd leaves, wither'd leaves, ye tell a mournful tale,

> Of love once true, and friends once kind,
> And happy moments fled:

> Dispersed by every breath of wind,
> Forgotten, changed, or dead!

Autumn leaves, autumn leaves, lie strewn around me here;
Autumn leaves, autumn leaves, how sad, how cold, how drear!

An hour past the old time, and still no Lucy! 'Tis useless lingering here: I'll wait no longer. A female crossing the meadow!—'Tis Rose, the bearer of a letter or a message perhaps.

Enter ROSE. (She avoids him.)

No! Then I will see Lucy at once, without a moment's delay. (Going.)

ROSE. No, no, you can't. (Aside.) There'll certainly be bloodshed! I am quite certain Mr. Flam will kill him. He offered me, with the most insinuating speeches, to cut John's throat at a moment's notice: and when the Squire complimented him on being a good shot, he said he should like to 'bag' the whole male population of the village. (To him.) You can't see her.

EDMUNDS. Not see her, and she at home! Were you instructed to say this, Rose?

ROSE. I say it, because I know you can't see her. She is not well; and—and—

EDMUNDS. And Mr. Norton is there, you would say.

ROSE. Mr. Norton!

EDMUNDS. Yes, Mr. Norton. Was he not there last evening? Was he not there the evening before? Is he not there at this moment?

Enter JOHN MADDOX.

JOHN. There at this moment?—of course he is.

ROSE. (aside). John here!

JOHN. Of course he is; of course he was there last night; and of course he was there the evening before. He's always there, and so is his bosom friend and confidential demon, Mr. Sparkins Flam. Oh! George, we're injured men, both of us.

EDMUNDS. Heartless girl! (Retires up.)

JOHN (to ROSE). Faithless person!

ROSE. Don't call me a person.

JOHN. You are a person, perjured, treacherous, and deceiving! Oh! George, if you had seen what I have seen to-day. Soft whisperings and loving smiles, gentle looks and encouraging sighs,—such looks and sighs as used once upon a time to be bestowed on us, George! If you had seen the Squire making up to Lucy, and Rose making up to Flam:—but I am very glad you did not see it, George, very. It would have broken your heart, as it has broken mine! Oh, Rose! could you break my heart?

ROSE. I could break your head with the greatest pleasure, you mischief-making booby; and if you don't make haste to wherever you're going, somebody that I know of will certainly do so, very quickly.

JOHN. Will he, will he?—your friend, Mr. Flam, I suppose! Let him—that's all; let him! (Retires up.)

ROSE. Oh! I'll let him: you needn't be afraid of my interfering. Dear, dear, I wish Mr. Flam would come, for I will own, notwithstanding what graver people may say, that I enjoy a little flirtation as much as any one.

Song.—ROSE.
> Some folks who have grown old and sour,
> Say love does nothing but annoy.
> The fact is, they have had their hour,
> So envy what they can't enjoy.
> I like the glance—I like the sigh—
> That does of ardent passion tell!
> If some folks were as young as I,
> I'm sure they'd like it quite as well.
> Old maiden aunts so hate the men,
> So well know how wives are harried,
> It makes them sad—not jealous—when
> They see their poor dear nieces married.
> All men are fair and false, they know,
> And with deep sighs they assail 'em,
> It's so long since they tried men, though,
> I rather think their memories fail 'em.

—Here comes Mr. Flam. You'd better go, John. I know you'll be murdered.

JOHN. Here I shall stop; let him touch me, and he shall feel the weight of my indignation.

Enter FLAM.

FLAM. Ah, my charmer! Punctual to my time, you see, my sweet little Damask Rose!

JOHN (coming down). A great deal more like a monthly one,—constantly changing, and gone the moment you wear it.

ROSE. Impertinent creature!

FLAM. Who is this poetical cauliflower?

JOHN. Don't pretend not to know me. You know who I am, well enough.

FLAM. As I live, it's the Ox!—retire, Ox, to your pasture, and don't rudely disturb the cooing of the doves. Go and graze, Ox!

JOHN. Suppose I choose to remain here, what then?

FLAM. Why then you must be driven off, mad Ox. (To ROSE.) Who is that other grasshopper?

ROSE. Hush, hush! for Heaven's sake don't let him hear you! It's young Edmunds.

FLAM. Young Edmunds? And who the devil is young Edmunds? For beyond the natural inference that young Edmunds is the son of old Edmunds, curse me if the fame of young Edmunds has ever reached my ears.

ROSE (in a low tone). It's Lucy's former lover, whom she has given up for the squire.

FLAM. The rejected cultivator?

ROSE. The same.

FLAM. Ah! I guessed as much from his earthy appearance. But, my darling Rose, I must speak with you,—I must—(putting his arm round her waist, sees JOHN). Good-bye, Ox!

JOHN. Good-bye!

FLAM. Pleasant walk to you, Ox!

JOHN. (not moving). Thank 'ee;—same to you!

FLAM. That other clodpole must not stay here either.

ROSE. Yes, yes! he neither sees nor hears us. Pray let him remain.

FLAM (to JOHN). You understand, Ox, that it is my wish that you forthwith retire and graze,—or in other words, that you at once, and without delay, betake yourself to the farm, or the devil, or any other place where you are in your element, and won't be in the way.

JOHN. Oh yes, I understand that.

FLAM. Very well; then the sooner you create a scarcity of such animals in this market, the better. Now, my dear Rose (puts his arm round her waist again). Are you gone, Ox?

JOHN. No.

FLAM. Are you going?

JOHN. By no means.

FLAM. This insolence is not to be borne.

ROSE. Oh, pray don't hurt him,—pray don't. Go away, you stupid creature, if you don't want to be ruined.

JOHN. That's just the very advice I would give you, Rose; do you go away, if you don't want to be ruined. As for me, this is a public place, and here I'll remain just as long as I think proper.

FLAM (quitting ROSE, and advancing towards him). You will?

JOHN. I will.

ROSE. Oh, dear, dear! I knew he'd be murdered all along. I was quite certain of it.

JOHN. Don't frown and scowl at me,—it won't do,—it only makes me smile; and when you talk of insolence and put my blood up, I tell you at once, that I am not to be bullied.

FLAM. Bullied?

JOHN. Ay, bullied was the word,—bullied by a coward, if you like that better.

FLAM. Coward! (Seizes his gun by the barrel, and aims a blow at him, with the butt-end; EDMUNDS rushes forward, and strikes it up with his stick.)

EDMUNDS. Hold your hand, sir,—hold your hand, or I'll fell you to the ground. Maddox, leave this place directly: take the opposite path, and I'll follow you. (Exit MADDOX.) As for you, sir, who by the way of vindicating yourself from the charge of cowardice, raise your gun against an unarmed man, tell your protector, the Squire, from me, that he and his companions might content themselves with turning the heads of our farmers' daughters, and endeavouring to corrupt their hearts, without wantonly insulting the men they have most injured. Let this be a lesson to you, sir,—although you were armed, you would have had the worst of a scuffle, and you may not have the benefit of a third person's interference at so critical a moment, another time;—remember this warning, sir, and benefit by it.

[Exit.

FLAM (aside). If Norton does not take a dear revenge for this insult, I have lost my influence with him. Bully! coward! They shall rue it.

ROSE (with her apron to her eyes). Oh, Mr. Flam! I can't bear to think that you should have suffered all this, on my account.

FLAM (aside). On her account!—a little vanity! (To her.) Suffered! Why, my dear, it was the drollest and most humorous affair that ever happened. Here stand I,—the Honourable Sparkins Flam,—on this second day of September, one thousand seven hundred and twenty-nine; and positively and solemnly declare that all the coffee-houses, play-houses, faro-tables, brag-tables, assemblies, drums and routs of a whole season put together, could not furnish such a splendid piece of exquisite drollery. The idea is admirable. My affecting to quarrel with a ploughman, and submitting to be lectured by another caterpillar, whom I suffer to burst into a butterfly importance!

ROSE. Then you were not really quarrelling?

FLAM. Bless you, no! I was only acting.

ROSE. Lor'! how well you do act, to be sure.

FLAM. Come, let us retire into the house, or after this joke we shall be the gaze of all the animated potatoes that are planted in this hole of a village. Why do you hesitate, Damask?

ROSE. Why, I have just been thinking that if you go to all these coffee-houses, and play-houses, and fairs, and brags, and keep playing drums, and routing people about, you'll forget me, when you go back to London.

FLAM (aside). More than probable. (To her.) Never fear; you will be generally known as Rose the lovely, and I shall be universally denominated Flam the constant.

Duet.—ROSE and SPARKINS FLAM.

FLAM.
'Tis true I'm caress'd by the witty,
The envy of all the fine beaux,
The pet of the court and the city,
But still I'm the lover of Rose.

ROSE.
Country sweethearts, oh, how I despise!
And oh! how delighted I am
To think that I shine in the eyes
Of the elegant—sweet—Mr. Flam.

FLAM. Allow me (offers to kiss her).

ROSE. Pray don't be so bold, sir. (Kisses her.)

FLAM. What sweets on that honey'd lip hang!

ROSE. Your presumption, I know, I should scold, sir,
But I really can't scold Mr. Flam.

BOTH.
Then let us be happy together,
Content with the world as it goes,
An unchangeable couple for ever,
Mr. Flam and his beautiful Rose.

[Exeunt.

SCENE III.—The Farmer's Kitchen. A table and chairs.

Enter OLD BENSON and MARTIN.

BENSON. Well, Stokes. Now you have the opportunity you have desired, and we are alone, I am ready to listen to the information which you wished to communicate to my private ear.

MARTIN. Exactly;—you said information, I think?

BENSON. You said information, or I have forgotten.

MARTIN. Just so, exactly; I said information. I did say information, why should I deny it?

BENSON. I see no necessity for your doing so, certainly. Pray go on.

MARTIN. Why, you see, my dear Mr. Benson, the fact is—won't you be seated? Pray sit down (brings forward two chairs;—they sit). There, now,—let me see,—where was I?

BENSON. You were going to begin, I think.

MARTIN. Oh,—ah!—so I was;—I hadn't begun, had I?

BENSON. No, no! Pray begin again, if you had.

MARTIN. Well, then, what I have got to say is not so much information, as a kind of advice, or suggestion, or hint, or something of that kind; and it relates to—eh?—(looking very mysterious.)

BENSON. What?

MARTIN. Yes (nodding). Don't you think there's something wrong there?

BENSON. Where?

MARTIN. In that quarter.

BENSON. In what quarter? Speak more plainly, sir.

MARTIN. You know what a friendly feeling I entertain to your family. You know what a very particular friend of mine you are. You know how anxious I always am to prevent anything going wrong.

BENSON. Well! (abruptly).

MARTIN. Yes, I see you're very sensible of it, but I'll take it for granted: you needn't bounce and fizz about, in that way, because it makes one nervous. Don't you think, now, don't you think, that ill-natured people may say;—don't be angry, you know, because if I wasn't a very particular friend of the family, I wouldn't mention the subject on any account;—don't you think that ill-natured people may say there's something wrong in the frequency of the Squire's visits here?

BENSON (starting up furiously). What!

MARTIN (aside). Here he goes again!

BENSON. Who dares suspect my child?

MARTIN. Ah, to be sure, that's exactly what I say. Who dares? Damme, I should like to see 'em!

BENSON. Is it you?

MARTIN. I! Bless you, no, not for the world! I!—Come, that's a good one. I only say what other people say, you know; that's all.

BENSON. And what are these tales, that idle busy fools prate of with delight, among themselves, caring not whose ears they reach, so long as they are kept from the old man, whose blindness—the blindness of a fond and doting father—is subject for their rude and brutal jeering. What are they?

MARTIN. Dear me, Mr. Benson, you keep me in a state of perpetual excitement.

BENSON. Tell me, without equivocation, what do they say?

MARTIN. Why, they say they think it—not exactly wrong, perhaps; don't fly out, now—but among those remarkable coincidences which do occur sometimes, that whenever you go out of your house, the Squire and his friend should come into it; that Miss Lucy and Miss Rose, in the long walks they take every day, should be met and walked home with by the same gentlemen; that long after you have gone to bed at night, the Squire and Mr. Sparkins Flam should still be seen hovering about the lane and meadow; and that one of the lattice windows should be always open, at that hour.

BENSON. This is all?

MARTIN. Ye—yes—yes, that's all.

BENSON. Nothing beside?

MARTIN. Eh?

BENSON. Nothing beside?

MARTIN. Why, there is something else, but I know you'll begin to bounce about again, if I tell it you.

BENSON. No, no! let me hear it all.

MARTIN. Why, then, they do say that the Squire has been heard to boast that he had practised on Lucy's mind—that when he bid her, she would leave her father and her home, and follow him over the world.

BENSON. They lie! Her breast is pure and innocent! Her soul is free from guilt; her mind from blemish. They lie! I'll not believe it. Are they mad? Do they think that I stand tamely by, and look upon my child's disgrace? Heaven! do they know of what a father's heart is made?

MARTIN. My dear Mr. Benson, if you—

BENSON. This coarse and brutal boast shall be disowned. (Going; MARTIN stops him.)

MARTIN. My dear Mr. Benson, you know it may not have been made after all,—my dear sir,—

BENSON (struggling). Unhand me, Martin! Made, or not made, it has gone abroad, fixing an infamous notoriety on me and mine. I'll hear its truth or falsehood from himself. (Breaks from him and exit.)

MARTIN (solus). There'll be something decidedly wrong here presently. Hallo! here's another very particular friend in a fume.

Enter YOUNG BENSON hastily.

MARTIN. Ah! my dear fellow, how—

YOUNG BENSON. Where is Lucy?

MARTIN. I don't know, unless she has walked out with the Squire.

YOUNG BENSON. The Squire!

MARTIN. To be sure; she very often walks out with the Squire. Very pleasant recreation walking out with the Squire; capital custom, an't it?

YOUNG BENSON. Where's my father?

MARTIN. Why, upon my word, I am unable to satisfy your curiosity in that particular either. All I know of him is that he whisked out of this room in a rather boisterous and turbulent manner for an individual at his time of life, some few seconds before you whisked in. But what's the matter?—you seem excited. Nothing wrong, is there?

YOUNG BENSON (aside). This treatment of Edmunds, and Lucy's altered behaviour to him, confirm my worst fears. Where is Mr. Norton?

MARTIN (calling off). Ah! to be sure,—where is Mr. Norton?

Enter SQUIRE.

SQUIRE. Mr. Norton is here. Who wishes to see him?

MARTIN. To be sure, sir. Mr. Norton is here: who wishes to see him?

YOUNG BENSON. I do.

MARTIN. I don't. Old fellow, good-bye! Mr. Norton, good evening! (Aside.) There'll be something wrong here, in a minute.

[Exit.

SQUIRE. Well, young man?

YOUNG BENSON. If you contemplate treachery here, Mr. Norton, look to yourself. My father is an old man; the chief prop of his declining years is his child,—my sister. For your actions here, sir, you shall render a dear account to me.

SQUIRE. To you, peasant!

YOUNG BENSON. To me, sir. One other scene like that enacted by your creature, at your command, to-night, may terminate more seriously to him. For your behaviour here you are responsible to me.

SQUIRE. Indeed! Anything more, sir?

YOUNG BENSON. Simply this:—after injuring the old man beyond reparation, and embittering the last moments of his life, you may possibly attempt to shield yourself under the paltry excuse, that, as a gentleman, you cannot descend to take the consequences from my hand. You shall take them from me, sir, if I strike you to the earth first.

[Exit.

SQUIRE. Fiery and valorous, indeed! As the suspicions of the family are aroused, no time is to be lost: the girl must be carried off to-night, if possible. With Flam's assistance and management, she may be speedily removed from within the reach of these rustic sparks. In my cooler moments, the reflection of the misery I may inflict upon the old man makes my conduct appear base and dishonourable, even to myself. Pshaw! hundreds have done the same thing before me, who have been lauded and blazoned forth as men of honour. Honour in such cases,—an idle tale!—a by-word! Honour! There is much to be gleaned from old tales; and the legend of the child and the old man speaks but too truly.

Song.—SQUIRE NORTON.
>   The child and the old man sat alone
>   In the quiet peaceful shade
>   Of the old green boughs, that had richly grown
>   In the deep thick forest glade.
>   It was a soft and pleasant sound,
>   That rustling of the oak;
>   And the gentle breeze play'd lightly round,
>   As thus the fair boy spoke:—
>
>   'Dear father, what can honour be,
>   Of which I hear men rave?
>   Field, cell and cloister, land and sea,
>   The tempest and the grave:—
>   It lives in all, 'tis sought in each,
>   'Tis never heard or seen:
>   Now tell me, father, I beseech,
>   What can this honour mean?'
>
>   'It is a name,—a name, my child,—
>   It lived in other days,
>   When men were rude, their passions wild,
>   Their sport, thick battle-frays.
>   When in armour bright, the warrior bold,
>   Knelt to his lady's eyes:
>   Beneath the abbey-pavement old
>   That warrior's dust now lies.
>
>   'The iron hearts of that old day
>   Have moulder'd in the grave;

And chivalry has pass'd away,
With knights so true and brave;
The honour, which to them was life,
Throbs in no bosom now;
It only gilds the gambler's strife,
Or decks the worthless vow.'

Enter LUCY.

SQUIRE. Lucy, dear Lucy.

LUCY. Let me entreat you not to stay here, sir! you will be exposed to nothing but insult and attack. Edmunds and my brother have both returned, irritated at something that has passed with my cousin Rose:—for my sake,—for my sake, Mr. Norton, spare me the pain of witnessing what will ensue, if they find you here. You little know what I have borne already.

SQUIRE. For your sake, Lucy, I would do much; but why should I leave you to encounter the passion and ill-will, from which you would have me fly?

LUCY. Oh, I can bear it, sir; I deserve it but too well.

SQUIRE. Deserve it!—you do yourself an injustice, Lucy. No; rather let me remove you from a house where you will suffer nothing but persecution, and confer upon you a title which the proudest lady in the land might wear. Here—here, on my knees (he bends on his knee, and seizes her hand.)

Enter FLAM.

SQUIRE (rising). Flam here!

FLAM (aside). Upon my word!—I thought we had been getting on pretty well in the open air, but they're beating us hollow here, under cover.

SQUIRE. Lucy, but one word, and I understand your decision.

LUCY. I—I—cannot subdue the feelings of uneasiness and distrust which the great difference between your honour's rank and mine awakens in my mind.

SQUIRE. Difference! Hundreds of such cases happen every day!

LUCY. Indeed!

SQUIRE. Oh, 'tis a matter of general notoriety,—isn't it, Flam?

FLAM. No doubt of it. (Aside.) Don't exactly know yet what they are talking about, though.

SQUIRE. A relation of my own, a man of exalted rank, courted a girl far his inferior in station but only beneath him in that respect. In all others she was on a footing of equality with himself, if not far above him.

LUCY. And were they married?

FLAM (aside). Rather an important circumstance in the case. I do remember that.

SQUIRE. They were,—after a time, when the resentment of his friends, occasioned by his forming such an attachment, had subsided, and he was able to acknowledge her, without involving the ruin of both.

LUCY. They were married privately at first, then?

FLAM (aside). I must put in a word here. Oh, yes, it was all comfortably arranged to everybody's satisfaction,—wasn't it, Norton?

SQUIRE. Certainly. And a happy couple they were, weren't they, Flam?

FLAM. Happiest of the happy. As happy as (aside)—a separation could make them.

SQUIRE. Hundreds of great people have formed similar attachments,—haven't they, Flam?

FLAM. Undoubtedly. There was the Right Honourable Augustus Frederick Charles Thomson Camharado, and the German Baron Hyfenstyfenlooberhausen, and they were both married—(aside) to somebody else, first. Not to mention Damask and I, who are models of constancy. By the bye, I have lost sight of her, and I am interrupting you. (Aside to SQUIRE, as he goes out.) I came to tell you that she is ripe for an elopement, if you urge her strongly. Edmunds has been reproaching her to my knowledge. She'll consent while her passion lasts.

[Exit

SQUIRE. Lucy, I wait your answer. One word from you, and a few hours will place you far beyond the reach of those who would fetter your choice and control your inclinations. You hesitate. Come, decide. The Squire's lady, or the wife of Edmunds!

Duet.—LUCY and SQUIRE NORTON.

SQUIRE.
In rich and lofty station shine,
Before his jealous eyes:
In golden splendour, lady mine,
This peasant youth despise.

LUCY (apart: the SQUIRE regarding her attentively).

Oh! It would be revenge indeed
With scorn his glance to meet.
I, I, his humble pleading heed!
I'd spurn him from my feet.

SQUIRE.
With love and rage her bosom's torn,
And rash the choice will be;

LUCY.
With love and rage my bosom's torn,
And rash the choice will be.

SQUIRE.
From hence she quickly must be borne,
Her home, her home, she'll flee.

LUCY.
Oh! long shall I have cause to mourn
My home, my home, for thee!

Enter OLD BENSON.

BENSON. What do I see! The Squire and Lucy.

SQUIRE. Listen. A chaise and four fleet horses, under the direction of a trusty friend of mine, will be in waiting on the high road, at the corner of the Elm-Tree avenue, to-night, at ten o'clock. They shall bear you whither we can be safe, and in secret, by the first light of morning.

LUCY. His cruel harshness;—it would be revenge, indeed. But my father—my poor old father!

SQUIRE. Your father is prejudiced in Edmund's favour; and so long as he thinks there is any chance of your being his, he will oppose your holding communication with me. Situated as you are now, you only stand in the way of his wealth and advancement. Once fly with me, and in four and twenty hours you will be his pride, his boast, his support.

OLD BENSON coming forward.

BENSON. It is a lie, a base lie!—(LUCY shrieks and throws herself at his feet.) My pride! my boast! She would be my disgrace, my shame: an outcast from her father's roof, and from the world. Support!—Support me with the gold coined in her infamy and guilt! Heaven help me! Have I cherished her for this!

LUCY (clinging to him). Father!—dear, dear, father!

SQUIRE. Hear me speak, Benson. Be calm.

BENSON. Calm!—Do you know that from infancy I have almost worshipped her, fancying that I saw in her young mind the virtues of a mother, to whom the anguish of this one hour would have been worse than death! Calm!—Do you know that I have a heart and soul within me; or do you believe that because I am of lower station, I am a being of a different order from yourself, and that Nature has denied me thought and feeling! Calm! Man, do you know that I am this girl's father?

SQUIRE. Benson, if you will not hear me, at least do not, by hastily exposing this matter, deprive me of the inclination of making you some reparation.

BENSON. Reparation! You need be thankful, sir, for the grasp she has upon my arm. Money! If she were dying for want, and the smallest coin from you could restore her to life and health, sooner than she should take it from your hand, I would cast her from a sick bed to perish on the road-side.

SQUIRE. Benson, a word.

BENSON. Do not, I caution you; do not talk to me, sir. I am an old man, but I do not know what passion may make me do.

SQUIRE. These are high words, Benson. A farmer!

BENSON. Yes, sir; a farmer, one of the men on whom you, and such as you, depend for the money they squander in profligacy and idleness. A farmer, sir! I care not for your long pedigree of ancestors,—my forefathers made them all. Here, neighbours, friends! (ROSE, MADDOX, STOKES, Villagers, etc., crowd on the stage.) Hear this, hear this! your landlord, a high-born gentleman, entering the houses of your humble farmers, and tempting their daughters to destruction!

Enter YOUNG BENSON and GEORGE EDMUNDS.

YOUNG BENSON. What's that I hear? (rushing towards the SQUIRE, STOKES interposes).

MARTIN. Hallo, hallo! Take hold of the other one, John. (MADDOX and he remove them to opposite sides of the stage.) Hold him tight, John, hold him tight. Stand still, there's a good fellow. Keep back, Squire. Knew there'd be something wrong,—ready to come in at the nick of time,—capital custom.

FLAM enters and stands next the SQUIRE.

SQUIRE. Exposed, baited! Benson, are you mad? Within the last few hours my friend here has been attacked and insulted on the very land you hold, by a person in your employ and young Edmunds there. I, too, have been threatened and insulted in the presence of my tenantry and workmen. Take care you do not drive me to extremities. Remember—the lease of this farm for seventy years, which your father took of mine, expires to-morrow; and that I have the power to refuse its renewal. Again I ask you, are you mad?

BENSON. Quit my house, villain!

SQUIRE. Villain! quit my house, then. This farm is mine: and you and yours shall depart from under its roof, before the sun has set to-morrow. (BENSON sinks into a chair in centre, and covers his face with his hands.)

Sestet and Chorus.

LUCY—ROSE—EDMUNDS—SQUIRE NORTON—FLAM—

YOUNG BENSON—and Chorus.

YOUNG BENSON. Turn him from the farm! From his home will you cast
        The old man who has till'd it for years?
        Every tree, every flower, is link'd with the past,
        And a friend of his childhood appears.

Turn him from the farm! O'er its grassy hill-side,
A gay boy he once loved to range;
His boyhood has fled, and its dear friends are dead,
But these meadows have never known change.

EDMUNDS.   Oppressor, hear me.

LUCY.   On my knees I implore

SQUIRE.   I command it, and you will obey.

ROSE.   Rise, dear Lucy, rise; you shall not kneel before
             The tyrant who drives us away.

SQUIRE.   Your sorrows are useless, your prayers are in vain;
             I command it and you will begone.
             I'll hear no more.

EDMUNDS.   No, they shall not beg again,
             Of a man whom I view with deep scorn.

FLAM.   Do not yield.

YOUNG BENSON /SQUIRE / LUCY / ROSE. Leave the farm!

EDMUNDS.   Your power I despise.

SQUIRE.   And your threats, boy, I disregard too.

FLAM.   Do not yield.

YOUNG BENSON /SQUIRE / LUCY / ROSE. Leave the farm!

ROSE.   If he leaves it, he dies.

EDMUNDS.   This base act, proud man, you shall rue.

YOUNG BENSON. Turn him from the farm! From his home will you cast
             The old man who has till'd it for years?
             Every tree, every flower, is linked with the past,
             And a friend of his childhood appears!

SQUIRE.   Yes, yes, leave the farm! From his home I will cast,
             The old man who has till'd it for years;
             Though each tree and flower is link'd with the past,
             And a friend of his childhood appears.

Chorus.   He has turn'd from his farm, from his home he has cast
             The old man who has till'd it for years;
             Though each tree and flower is link'd with the past,
             And a friend of his childhood appears.

END OF THE FIRST ACT

ACT II.

SCENE I.—An Apartment in the Hall. A breakfast-table, with urn and tea-service. A Livery Servant arranging it. FLAM in a morning gown and slippers, reclining on the sofa.

FLAM. Is the Squire out of bed yet?

SERVANT. Yes, sir, he will be down directly.

FLAM. Any letters from London?

SERVANT. One for your honour, that the man brought over from the market-town, this morning.

FLAM. Give it me, blockhead! (Servant gives it, and exit.) Never like the look of a great official-folded letter, with a large seal, it's always an unpleasant one. Talk of discovering a man's character from his handwriting!—I'll back myself against any odds to form a very close guess at the contents of a letter from the form into which it is folded. This, now, I should say, is a decidedly hostile fold. Let us see— 'King's Bench Walk—September 1st, 1729. Sir, I am instructed by my client, Mr. Edward Montague, to apply to you—(the old story—for the immediate payment, I suppose—what's this?)—to apply to you for the instant restitution of the sum of two hundred and fifty pounds, his son lost to you at play; and to acquaint you, that unless it is immediately forwarded to my office, as above, the circumstances of the transaction will be made known; and the unfair and fraudulent means by which you deprived the young man of his money, publicly advertised.—I am, Sir, your obedient Servant, John Ellis.' The devil! who would believe now, that such a trifling circumstance as the mere insinuation of a small piece of gold into the corner of two dice would influence a man's destiny! What's to be done? If, by some dexterous stroke, I could manage to curry favour with Norton, and procure some handsome present in return for services rendered,—for 'work and labour done and performed,' as my obedient servant, John Ellis, would say, I might keep my head above water yet. I have it! He shall have a joyful surprise. I'll carry this girl off for him, and he shall know nothing of the enterprise until it is completed, or at least till she is fairly off. I have been well rewarded for similar services before, and may securely calculate on his gratitude in the present instance. He is here. (Puts up the letter.)

Enter SQUIRE NORTON.

SQUIRE (seating himself at table). Has any application for permission to remain on the farm been made from Benson, this morning, Flam?

FLAM. None.

SQUIRE. I am very sorry for it, although I admire the old man's independent spirit. I am very sorry for it. Wrong as I know I have been, I would rather that the first concession came from him.

FLAM. Concession!

SQUIRE. The more I reflect upon the occurrences of yesterday, Flam, the more I regret that, under the influence of momentary passion and excitement, I should have used so uncalled-for a threat against my father's oldest tenant. It is an act of baseness to which I look back with abhorrence.

FLAM (aside). What weathercock morality is this!

SQUIRE. It was unnecessary violence.

FLAM. Unnecessary! Oh, certainly; no doubt you could have attained your object without it, and can still. There is no occasion to punish the old man.

SQUIRE. Nor will I. He shall not leave the farm, if I myself implore, and beg him to remain.

Enter Servant.

SERVANT. Two young women to speak with your honour.

Enter LUCY and ROSE.

SQUIRE. Lucy!

FLAM (aside). She must be carried off to-night, or she certainly will save me the trouble, and I shall lose the money.

LUCY. Your honour may be well surprised to see me here, after the events of yesterday. It has cost me no trifling struggle to take this step, but I hope my better feelings have at length prevailed, and conquered my pride and weakness. I wish to speak to your honour, with nobody by.

FLAM (aside). Nobody by! I rather suspect I'm not particularly wanted here. (To them.) Pray allow us to retire for a few moments. Rose, my dear.

ROSE. Well!

FLAM. Come along.

LUCY. Rose will remain here, I brought her for that purpose.

FLAM. Bless me! that's very odd. As you please, of course, but I really think you'll find her very much in the way. (Aside.) Acting propriety! So much the better for my purpose; a little coyness will enhance the value of the prize.

[Exit FLAM.

LUCY. Mr. Norton, I come here to throw myself upon your honourable feelings, as a man and as a gentleman. Oh, sir! now that my eyes are opened to the misery into which I have plunged myself, by my own ingratitude and treachery, do not—do not add to it the reflection that I have driven my father in his old age from the house where he was born, and in which he hoped to have died.

SQUIRE. Be calm, Lucy; your father shall continue to hold the farm; the lease shall be renewed.

LUCY. I have more to say to your honour still, and what I have to add may even induce your honour to retract the promise you have just now made me.

SQUIRE. Lucy! what can you mean?

LUCY. Oh, sir! call me coquette, faithless, treacherous, deceitful, what you will; I deserve it all;—but believe me, I speak the truth when I make the humiliating avowal. A weak, despicable vanity induced me to listen with a ready ear to your honour's addresses, and to cast away the best and noblest heart that ever woman won.

SQUIRE. Lucy, 'twas but last night you told me that your love for Edmunds had vanished into air; that you hated and despised him.

LUCY. I know it, sir, too well. He laid bare my own guilt, and showed me the ruin which impended over me. He spoke the truth. Your honour more than confirmed him.

SQUIRE (after a pause). Even the avowal you have just made, unexpected as it is, shall not disturb my resolution. Your father shall not leave the farm.

Quartet.

LUCY / ROSE / SQUIRE NORTON, and afterwards YOUNG BENSON.

| SQUIRE. | Hear me, when I swear that the farm is your own
Through all changes Fortune may make;
The base charge of falsehood I never have known;
This promise I never will break. |
| ROSE and LUCY. | Hear him, when he swears that the farm is our own
Through all changes Fortune may make;
The base charge of falsehood he never has known;
This promise he never will break. |

Enter YOUNG BENSON.

YOUNG BENSON. My sister here! Lucy! begone, I command.

SQUIRE. To your home I restore you again.

YOUNG BENSON. No boon I'll accept from that treacherous hand
As the price of my sister's fair fame.

SQUIRE. To your home!

YOUNG BENSON (to LUCY.) Hence away!

LUCY. Brother dear, I obey.

SQUIRE. I restore.

YOUNG BENSON. Hence away!

YOUNG BENSON, ROSE and LUCY. Let us leave.

LUCY. He swears it, dear brother.

SQUIRE.	I swear it.
YOUNG BENSON.	Away!
SQUIRE.	I swear it.
YOUNG BENSON.	You swear to deceive.
SQUIRE.	Hear me, when I swear that the farm is your own Through all changes Fortune may make.
LUCY and ROSE.	Hear him when he swears that the farm is our own. Through all changes Fortune may make.
YOUNG BENSON.	Hear him swear, hear him swear, that the farm is our own Through all changes Fortune may make.
SQUIRE.	The base charge of falsehood I never have known, This promise I never will break.
LUCY and ROSE.	The base charge of falsehood he never has known, This promise he never will break.
YOUNG BENSON.	The base charge of falsehood he often has known This promise he surely will break.

[Exeunt omnes.

Re-enter FLAM, in a walking-dress.

FLAM. The coast is clear at last. What on earth the conversation can have been, at which Rose was wanted, and I was not, I confess my inability to comprehend; but away with speculation, and now to business.—(Rings.)

Enter Servant.

Pen and ink.

SERVANT. Yes, sir.

[Exit Servant.

FLAM (solus). Nearly all the tenantry will be assembled here at the ball to-night; and if the father of this rustic Dulcinea is reinstated in his farm, he and his people will no doubt be among the number. It will be easy enough to entice the girl into the garden, through the window opening on the lawn; a chaise can be waiting in the quiet lane at the side, and some trusty fellow can slip a hasty note into Norton's hands informing him of the flight, and naming the place at which he can join us. (Re-enter Servant with pen, ink, taper and two sheets of notepaper; he places them on the table and exit.) I may as well reply to my friend Mr. John Ellis's obliging favour now, too, by promising that the money shall be forwarded in the course of three days' post. (Takes the letter from his pocket, and lays it on the table.) Lie you there. First, for Norton's note.—'Dear Norton,—knowing your wishes—seized the girl—no blame attach to you. Join us as soon as people have dispersed in search of her in all directions but the right one,—fifteen miles off.' (Folds it ready for an envelope and lays it by the side of the other letter.) Now for John Ellis. Why, what does the rascal mean by bringing but two sheets of paper? No matter: that affair will keep cool till to-morrow, when I have less business on my hands, and more money in my pockets, I hope. (Crumples the letter he has just written, hastily up, thrusts it into his pocket, and folds the wrong one in the envelope. As he is sealing it

Enter MARTIN, very cautiously.

MARTIN (peeping). There he is, hatching some mysterious and diabolical plot. If I can only get to the bottom of these dreadful designs, I shall immortalise myself. What a lucky dog I am, to be such a successful gleaner of news, and such a confidential person into the bargain, as to be the first to hear that he wanted some trustworthy person. All comes of talking to everybody I meet, and drawing out everything they hear. Capital custom! He don't see me. Hem! (Coughs very loud, and when FLAM looks round, nods familiarly.) How are you again?

FLAM. How am I again! Who the devil are you?—and what do you want here?

MARTIN. Hush!

FLAM. Eh?

MARTIN. Hush! I'm the man.

FLAM. The man!

MARTIN. Yes, the man that you asked the ostler at the George to recommend you; the trustworthy man that knows all the by-roads well, and can keep a secret; the man that you wanted to lend you a hand in a job that—

FLAM. Hush, hush!

MARTIN. Oh! you're beginning to hush now, are you?

FLAM. Haven't I seen your face before?

MARTIN. To be sure you have. You recollect admiring my manners at Benson's yesterday. You must remember Mr. Martin Stokes. You can't have forgotten him—not possible!

FLAM (aside). A friend of Benson!—a dangerous rencontre. Another moment, and our conversation might have taken an awkward turn. (To him.) So you are Stokes, eh? Benson's friend Stokes?

MARTIN. To be sure. Ha, ha! I knew you couldn't have forgotten me. Pleasant Stokes they call me, clever Stokes sometimes;—but that's flattery.

FLAM. No, surely.

MARTIN. Yes, 'pon my life! it is. Can't bear flattery,—don't like it at all.

FLAM. Well, Mr. Stokes—

MARTIN (aside). Now for the secret.

FLAM. I am very sorry you have had the trouble of coming up here, Mr. Stokes, because I have changed my plan, and shall not require your valuable services. (Goes up to the table.)

MARTIN (aside). Something wrong here: try him again. You're sure you don't want me?

FLAM. Quite.

MARTIN. That's unlucky, because, as I have quarrelled with Benson—

FLAM. Quarrelled with Benson!

MARTIN. What! didn't you know that?

FLAM. Never heard of it. Now I think of it, Mr. Stokes, I shall want your assistance. Pray, sit down, Mr. Stokes.

MARTIN. With pleasure. (They sit.) I say, I thought you wanted me.

FLAM. Ah! you're a sharp fellow.

MARTIN. You don't mean that?

FLAM. I do, indeed.

MARTIN (aside). You would, if you knew all.

FLAM (aside). Conceited hound!

MARTIN (aside). Poor devil!

FLAM. Mr. Stokes, I needn't impress upon a gentleman of your intelligence, the necessity of secrecy in this matter.

MARTIN. Of course not: see all—say nothing. Capital custom:—(aside) not mine though. Go on.

FLAM. You wouldn't mind playing Benson a trick,—just a harmless trick?

MARTIN. Certainly not. Go on.

FLAM. I'll trust you.

MARTIN. So you may. Go on.

FLAM. A chaise and four will be waiting to-night, at ten o'clock precisely, at the little gate that opens from the garden into the lane.

MARTIN. No: will it though? Go on.

FLAM. Don't interrupt me, Stokes. Into that chaise you must assist me in forcing as quickly as possible and without noise—

MARTIN. Yes. Go on.

FLAM. Whom do you think?

MARTIN. Don't know.

FLAM. Can't you guess whom?

MARTIN. No.

FLAM. Try.

MARTIN. Eh! what!—Miss—

FLAM. Hush, hush! You understand me, I see. Not another word; not another syllable.

MARTIN. But do you really mean to run away with—

FLAM (stopping his mouth). You understand me;—that's quite sufficient.

MARTIN (aside). He's going to run away with Rose. Why if I hadn't found this out, John Maddox,—one of my most particular friends,—would have gone stark, staring, raving mad with grief. (To him.) But what will become of Miss Lucy, when she has lost Rose?

FLAM. No matter. We cannot take them both, without the certainty of an immediate discovery. Meet me at the corner of the avenue, before the ball commences, and I will communicate any further instructions I may have to give you. Meanwhile take this (gives him money) as an earnest of what you shall receive when the girl is secured. Remember, silence and secrecy.

MARTIN. Silence and secrecy, (exit FLAM)—confidence and two guineas. I am perfectly bewildered with this tremendous secret. What shall I do? Where shall I go?—To my particular friend, old Benson, or young Benson, or George Edmunds? or—no; I'll go and paralyse my particular friend, John Maddox. Not a moment is to be lost. I am all in a flutter. Run away with Rose! I suppose he'll run away with Lucy next. I shouldn't wonder. Run away with Rose! I never did—

[Exit hastily.

SCENE II.—An open spot in the Village.

Enter SQUIRE NORTON.

SQUIRE. My mind is made up. This girl has opened her whole heart to me; and it would be worse than villainy to pursue her further. I will seek out Benson and Edmunds, and endeavour to repair the mischief my folly has occasioned. I have sought happiness in the dissipation of crowded cities, in vain. A country life offers health and cheerfulness; and a country life shall henceforth be mine, in all seasons.

Song.—SQUIRE NORTON.
    There's a charm in Spring, when everything
    Is bursting from the ground;

When pleasant showers bring forth the flowers,
And all is life around.

In summer day, the fragrant hay
Most sweetly scents the breeze;
And all is still, save murmuring rill,
Or sound of humming bees.

Old Autumn come, with trusty gun
In quest of birds we roam:
Unerring aim, we mark the game,
And proudly bear it home.

A winter's night has its delight,
Well warm'd to bed we go;
A winter's day, we're blithe and gay,
Snipe-shooting in the snow.

A country life without the strife
And noisy din of town,
Is all I need, I take no heed
Of splendour or renown.

And when I die, oh, let me lie
Where trees above me wave;
Let wild plants bloom, around my tomb,
My quiet country grave!

[Exit.

SCENE III.—The Rick-yard. Same as ACT I. SCENE I.

EDMUNDS and MADDOX meeting.

JOHN. Ah, George! Why this is kind to come down to the old farm to-day, and take one peep at us, before we leave it for ever. I suppose it's fancy, now, George, but to my thinking I never saw the hedges look so fresh, the fields so rich, or the old house so pretty and comfortable, as they do this morning. It's fancy that, George,—an't it?

EDMUNDS. It's a place you may well be fond of, and attached to, for it's the prettiest spot in all the country round.

JOHN. Ah! you always enter into my feelings; and speaking of that, I want to ask your advice about Rose. I meant to come up to you to-day, on purpose. Do you think she is fond of me, George?

EDMUNDS (smiling). What do you think? She has not shown any desperate warmth of affection, of late, has she?

JOHN. No—no, she certainly has not, but she used to once, and the girl has got a good heart after all; and she came crying to me, this morning, in the little paddock, and somehow or other, my heart melted towards her; and—and—there's something very pleasant about her manner,—isn't there, George?

EDMUNDS. No doubt of it, as other people besides ourselves would appear to think.

JOHN. You mean Mr. Flam? (EDMUNDS nods assent.) Ah! it's a bad business, altogether; but still there are some excuses to be made for a young country girl, who has never seen a town gentleman before, and can't be expected to know as well as you and I, George, what the real worth of one is. However that may be, Rose came into the little paddock this morning, as I was standing there, looking at the young colts, and thinking of all our misfortunes; and first of all she walked by me, and then she stopped at a little distance, and then she walked back, and stopped again; and I heard her sobbing as if her heart would burst: and then she came a little nearer, and at last she laid her hand upon my arm, and looked up in my face: and the tears started into my eyes, George, and I couldn't bear it any longer, for I thought of the many pleasant days we had been happy together, and it hurt me to think that she should ever have done anything to make her afraid of me, or me unkind to her.

EDMUNDS. You're a good fellow, John, an excellent fellow. Take her; I believe her to have an excellent disposition, though it is a little disguised by girlish levity sometimes;—you may safely take her,—if she had far less good feeling than she actually possesses, she could never abuse your kind and affectionate nature.

JOHN. Is that your advice? give me your hand, George (they shake hands), I will take her. You shall dance at our wedding, and I don't quite despair yet of dancing at yours, at the same time.

EDMUNDS. At mine! Where is the old man? I came here to offer him the little cottage in the village, which belongs to me. There is no tenant in it now: it has a pretty garden, of which I know he is fond, and it may serve his turn till he has had time to look about him.

JOHN. He is somewhere about the farm; walk with me across the yard, and perhaps we may meet him—this way.

[Exeunt.

Enter YOUNG BENSON.

YOUNG BENSON. The worst portion of the poor old man's hard trial is past. I have lingered with him in every field on the land, and wandered through every room in the old house. I can neither blame his grief, nor console him in his affliction, for the farm has been the happy scene of my birth and boyhood; and I feel, in looking on it, for the last time, as if I were leaving the dearest friends of my youth, for ever.

Song.—YOUNG BENSON.
     My fair home is no longer mine;

From its roof-tree I'm driven away,
Alas! who will tend the old vine,
Which I planted in infancy's day!
The garden, the beautiful flowers,
The oak with its branches on high,
Dear friends of my happiest hours,
Among ye, I long hoped to die.
The briar, the moss, and the bramble,
Along the green paths will run wild:
The paths where I once used to ramble,
An innocent, light-hearted child.

At the conclusion of the song enter to the symphony OLD BENSON, with LUCY and ROSE.

YOUNG BENSON (advancing to meet him). Come, father, come!

OLD BENSON. I am ready, boy. We have but to walk a few steps, and the pang of leaving is over. Come, Rose, bring on that unhappy girl; come!

As they are going, enter the SQUIRE, who meets them.

SQUIRE. I am in time.

BENSON (to YOUNG BENSON, who is advancing). Harry, stand back. Mr. Norton, if by this visit you intend to mock the misery you have inflicted here, it is a heartless insult that might have been spared.

SQUIRE. You do me an injustice, Benson. I come here,—not to insult your grief, but to entreat, implore you, to remain. The lease of this farm shall be renewed;—I beseech you to remain here.

BENSON. It is not the quitting even the home of my infancy, which most men love, that bows my spirit down to-day. Here, in this old house, for near two hundred years, my ancestors have lived and died, and left their names behind them free from spot or blemish. I am the first to cross its threshold with the brand of infamy upon me. Would to God I had been borne from its porch a senseless corpse many weary years ago, so that I had been spared this hard calamity! You have moved an old man's weakness, but not with your revenge, sir. You implore me to remain here. I spurn your offer. Here! A father yielding to the destroyer of his child's good name and honour! Say no more, sir. Let me pass.

Enter, behind, STOKES and EDMUNDS.

SQUIRE. Benson, you are guilty of the foulest injustice, not to me, but to your daughter. After her fearless confession to me this morning of her love for Edmunds, and her abhorrence of my professions, I honour her too much to injure her, or you.

LUCY. Dear father, it is true indeed. The noble behaviour of his honour to me, this morning, I can never forget, or be too grateful for.

BENSON. Thank God! thank God! I can look upon her once again. My child! my own child! (he embraces her with great emotion.) I have done your honour wrong, and I hope you'll forgive me. (They shake hands.)

MARTIN (running forward). So have I! so have I! I have done his honour wrong, and I hope he'll forgive me too. You don't leave the farm, then? Hurrah! (A man carrying a pail, some harness, etc., crosses the stage.) Hallo, young fellow! go back, go back! don't take another thing away, and bring back all you have carried off; they are going to stop in the farm. Hallo! you fellows! (Calling off.) Leave the barn alone, and put everything in its place. They are going to stop in the farm.

[Exit bawling.

BENSON (seeing EDMUNDS). What! George here, and turning away from his old friend, too, without a look of congratulation or a shake of the hand, just at the time, when of all others, he had the best right to expect it! For shame, George, for shame!

EDMUNDS. My errand here is rendered useless. By accident, and not intentionally, I partly overheard just now the nature of the avowal made by your daughter to Mr. Norton this morning.

BENSON. You believe it, George. You cannot doubt its truth.

EDMUNDS. I do believe it. But I have been hurt, slighted, set aside for another. My honest love has been despised; my affection has been remembered, only to be tried almost beyond endurance. Lucy, all this from you I freely forgive. Be what you have been once, and what you may so well become again. Be the high-souled woman; not the light and thoughtless trifler that disgraces the name. Let me see you this, and you are mine again. Let me see you what you have been of late, and I never can be yours!

BENSON. Lead her in, Rose. Come, dear, come! (The BENSONS and ROSE lead her slowly away.)

EDMUNDS. Mr. Norton, if this altered conduct be sincere, it deserves a much better return than my poor thanks can ever be to you. If it be feigned, to serve some purposes of your own, the consequences will be upon your head.

SQUIRE. And I shall be prepared to meet them.

Duet.—SQUIRE NORTON and EDMUNDS.

SQUIRE.   Listen, though I do not fear you,
              Listen to me, ere we part.

EDMUNDS.   List to you! Yes, I will hear you.

SQUIRE.   Yours alone is Lucy's heart,
              I swear it, by that Heaven above me.

EDMUNDS.   What! can I believe my ears!
              Could I hope that she still loves me!

SQUIRE.   Banish all these doubts and fears,
          If a love were e'er worth gaining,
          If love were ever fond and true,
          No disguise or passion feigning,
          Such is her young love for you.

          Listen, though I do not fear you,
          Listen to me ere we part.

EDMUNDS. List to you! yes, I will hear you,
          Mine alone is her young heart.

[Exeunt severally.

SCENE IV.—The avenue leading to the Hall, by moonlight.

The house in the distance, gaily illuminated.

Enter FLAM and MARTIN.

FLAM. You have got the letter I gave you for the Squire?

MARTIN. All right. Here it is.

FLAM. The moment you see me leave the room, slip it into the Squire's hand; you can easily do so, without being recognised, in the confusion of the dance, and then follow me. You perfectly understand your instructions?

MARTIN. Oh, yes,—I understand them well enough.

FLAM. There's nothing more, then, that you want to know?

MARTIN. No, nothing,—oh, yes there is. I want to know whether—whether—

FLAM. Well, go on.

MARTIN. Whether you could conveniently manage to let me have another couple of guineas, before you go away in the chaise. Payment beforehand,—capital custom. And if you don't, perhaps I may not get them at all, you know: (aside) seeing that I don't intend to go at all, I think it's very likely.

FLAM. You're a remarkably pleasant fellow, Stokes, in general conversation,—very,—but when you descend into particularities, you become excessively prosy. On some points,—money-matters for instance,—you have a very grasping imagination, and seem disposed to dilate upon them at too great a length. You must cure yourself of this habit,—you must indeed. Good-bye, Stokes; you shall have the two guineas doubled when the journey is completed. Remember,—ten o'clock.

[Exit FLAM.

MARTIN. I shan't forget ten o'clock, depend upon it. Now to burst upon my particular friend, Mr. John Maddox, with the awful disclosure. He must pass this way on his road to the Hall. Here they come,—don't see him though. (Groups of male and female Villagers in cloaks, etc., cross the stage on their way to the Hall.)

MARTIN. How are you, Tom? How do, Will?

VILLAGERS. How do, Mas'r Stokes?

MARTIN (shaking hands with them). How do, Susan? Mind, Cary, you're my first partner. Always kiss your first partner,—capital custom. (Kisses her.) Good-bye! See you up at the Hall.

VILLAGERS. Ay, ay, Mas'r Stokes.

[Exeunt Villagers.

MARTIN. Not among them. (More Villagers cross.) Nor them. Here he comes:—Rose with him too,— innocent little victim, little thinking of the atrocious designs that are going on against her!

Enter MADDOX and ROSE, arm-in-arm.

JOHN. Ha, ha, ha! that was a good 'un,—wasn't it? Ah! Martin, I wish I'd seen you a minute ago. I made such a joke! How you would ha' laughed!

MARTIN (mysteriously beckoning MADDOX away from ROSE, and whispering). I want to speak to you.

JOHN (whispering). What about?

ROSE. Lor'! don't stand whispering there, John. If you have anything to say, Mr. Stokes, say it before me.

JOHN (taking her arm). Ah! say it before her! Don't mind her, Martin; she's to be my wife, you know, and we're to be on the mutual-confidence principle; an't we,—Rose?

ROSE. To be sure. Why don't you speak, Mr. Stokes? I suppose it's the old story,—something wrong.

MARTIN. Something wrong! I rather think there is; and you little know what it is, or you wouldn't look so merry. What I have got to say—don't be frightened, Miss Rose,—relates to—don't alarm yourself, Master Maddox.

JOHN. I an't alarming myself; you're alarming me. Go on!

ROSE. Go on!—can't you?

MARTIN. Relates to Mr. Flam.

JOHN (dropping ROSE'S arm). Mr. Flam!

MARTIN. Hush!—and Miss Rose.

ROSE. Me! Me and Mr. Flam!

MARTIN. Mr. Flam intends at ten o'clock, this very night,—don't be frightened, Miss,—by force, in secret, and in a chaise and four, too,—to carry off, against her will, and elope with, Miss Rose.

ROSE. Me! Oh! (Screams, and falls into the arms of MADDOX.)

JOHN. Rub her hands, Martin, she's going off in a fit.

MARTIN. Never mind; she'd better go off in a fit than a chaise.

ROSE (recovering). Oh, John! don't let me go.

JOHN. Let you go!—not if I set the whole Hall on fire.

ROSE. Hold me fast, John.

JOHN. I'll hold you fast enough, depend upon it.

ROSE. Come on the other side of me, Mr. Stokes: take my arm; hold me tight, Mr. Stokes.

MARTIN. Don't be frightened, I'll take care of you. (Takes her arm.)

ROSE. Oh! Mr. Stokes.

MARTIN. Oh, indeed! Nothing wrong,—eh?

ROSE. Oh! Mr. Stokes,—pray forgive my having doubted that there was—Oh! what a dreadful thing! What is to be done with me?

MARTIN. Upon my word, I don't know. I think we had better shut her up in some place under ground,—hadn't we, John?—or, stay,—suppose we borrow the keys of the family vault, and lock her up there, for an hour or two.

JOHN. Capital!

ROSE. Lor'! surely you may find out some more agreeable place than that, John.

MARTIN. I have it.—I'm to carry her off.

BOTH. You!

MARTIN. Me,—don't be afraid of me:—all my management. You dance with her all the evening, and I'll keep close to you. If anybody tries to get her away, you knock him down,—and I'll help you.

JOHN. That's the plan;—come along.

ROSE. Oh, I am so frightened! Hold me fast, Mr. Stokes,—Don't let me go, John!

[Exeunt, talking.

Enter LUCY.

LUCY. Light-hearted revellers! how I envy them! How painful is my situation,—obliged with a sad heart to attend a festivity, from which the only person I would care to meet will, I know, be absent.

But I will not complain. He shall see that I can become worthy of him, once again. I have lingered here so long, watching the soft shades of evening as they closed around me, that I cannot bear the thought of exchanging this beautiful scene for the noise and glare of a crowded room.

Song.—LUCY.

> How beautiful at even-tide
> To see the twilight shadows pale,
> Steal o'er the landscape, far and wide,
> O'er stream and meadow, mound and dale.
> How soft is Nature's calm repose
> When evening skies their cool dews weep:
> The gentlest wind more gently blows,
> As if to soothe her in her sleep!
> The gay morn breaks,
> Mists roll away,
> All Nature awakes
> To glorious day.
> In my breast alone
> Dark shadows remain;
> The peace it has known
> It can never regain.

SCENE THE LAST.—A spacious ball-room, brilliantly illuminated. A window at the end, through which is seen a moonlit landscape. A large concourse of country people, discovered.—The SQUIRE,—FLAM,—the BENSONS,—LUCY,—ROSE,—MARTIN, and MADDOX.

SQUIRE. Welcome, friends, welcome all! Come, choose your partners, and begin the dance.

FLAM (to LUCY) Your hand, for the dance?

LUCY. Pray excuse me, sir; I am not well. My head is oppressed and giddy. I would rather sit by the window which looks into the garden, and feel the cool evening air. (She goes up. He follows her.)

JOHN (aside). Stand by me, Martin. He's gone to order the chaise, perhaps.

ROSE. Oh! pray don't let me be taken away, Mr. Stokes.

MARTIN. Don't be frightened,—don't be frightened. Mr. Flam is gone. I'll give the Squire the note in a minute.

SQUIRE. Now,—begin the dance.

A Country Dance.

(MARTIN and MADDOX, in their endeavours to keep close to ROSE, occasion great confusion. As the SQUIRE is looking at some particular couple in the dance, MARTIN steals behind him, thrusts the letter in his hands, and resumes his place. The SQUIRE looks round as if to discover the person who has delivered it; but being unsuccessful, puts it up, and retires among the crowd of dancers.

Suddenly a violent scream is heard, and the dance abruptly ceases. Great confusion. MARTIN and MADDOX hold Rose firmly.)

SQUIRE. What has happened? Whence did that scream proceed?

SEVERAL VOICES. From the garden!—from the garden!

EDMUNDS (without). Raise him, and bring him here. Lucy,—dear Lucy!

BENSON. Lucy! My child! (Runs up the stage, and exit into garden.)

MARTIN. His child! Damme! they can't get this one, so they're going to run away with the other. Here's some mistake here. Let me go, Rose. Come along, John. Make way there,—make way!

(As they run towards the window, EDMUNDS appears at it, without a hat, and his dress disordered, with LUCY in his arms. He delivers her to her father and ROSE.)

ROSE. Lucy,—dear Lucy,—look up!

BENSON. Is she hurt, George?—is the poor child injured?

EDMUNDS. No, it is nothing but terror; she will be better instantly. See! she is recovering now. (LUCY gradually recovers, as FLAM, his clothes torn, and face disfigured, is led in by MADDOX and MARTIN.)

BENSON. Mr. Norton, this is an act of perjury and baseness, of which another instant would have witnessed the completion.

SQUIRE (to FLAM). Rascal! this is your deed.

FLAM (aside to NORTON). That's right, Norton, keep it up.

SQUIRE. Do not address me with your odious familiarity, scoundrel!

FLAM. You don't really mean to give me up?

SQUIRE. I renounce you from this instant.

FLAM. You do?—then take the consequences.

SQUIRE. Benson,—Edmunds,—friends,—I declare to you most solemnly that I had neither hand nor part in this disgraceful outrage. It has been perpetrated without my knowledge, wholly by that scoundrel.

FLAM. 'Tis false; it was done with his consent. He has in his pocket, at this moment, a letter from me, acquainting him with my intention.

ALL. A letter!

SQUIRE. A letter was put into my hands five minutes since; but it acquainted me, not with this fellow's intention, but with his real dishonourable and disgraceful character, to which I had hitherto been a stranger. (To FLAM.) Do you know that handwriting, sir? (Showing him the letter.)

FLAM. Ellis's letter! (searching his pockets, and producing the other). I must,—ass that I was!—I did—enclose the wrong one.

SQUIRE. You will quit my house this instant; its roof shall not shelter you another night. Take that with you, sir, and begone. (Throws him a purse.)

FLAM (taking it up). Ah! I suppose you think this munificent, now—eh? I could have made twice as much of you in London, Norton, I could indeed, to say nothing of my exhibiting myself for a whole week to these clods of earth, which would have been cheap, dirt-cheap, at double the money. Bye-bye, Norton! Farewell, grubs!

[Exit.

SQUIRE. Edmunds, you have rescued your future wife from brutal violence; you will not leave her exposed to similar attempts in future?

EDMUNDS. Even if I would, I feel, now that I have preserved her, that I could not.

SQUIRE. Then take her, and with her the old farm, which from henceforth is your own. You will not turn the old man out, I suppose?

EDMUNDS (shaking BENSON by the hand). I don't think we are very likely to quarrel on that score; and most gratefully do we acknowledge your honour's kindness. Maddox!

JOHN. Hallo!

EDMUNDS. I shall not want that cottage and garden we were speaking of, this morning, now. Let me imitate a good example, and bestow it on your wife, as her marriage portion.

ROSE. Oh, delightful! Say certainly, John,—can't you?

JOHN. Thank 'ee, George, thank 'ee! I say, Martin, I have arrived at the dignity of a cottage and a piece of ground, at last.

MARTIN. Yes, you may henceforth consider yourself on a level with me.

SQUIRE. Resume the dance.

MARTIN. I beg your pardon. One word. (Whispers the SQUIRE.)

SQUIRE. I hope not. Recollect, you have been mistaken before, to-day. You had better inquire.

MARTIN. I will. (To the audience.) My very particular friend, if he will allow me to call him so,—

SQUIRE. Oh, certainly.

MARTIN. My very particular friend, Mr. Norton, wishes me to ask my other particular friends here, whether there's—anything wrong? We are delighted to hear your approving opinion in the old way. You can't do better. It's a capital custom.

Dance and Finale.—Chorus.
            Join the dance, with step as light

As every heart should be to-night;
Music, shake the lofty dome,
In honour of our Harvest Home.

Join the dance, and banish care,
All are young, and gay, and fair;
Even age has youthful grown,
In honour of our Harvest Home.

Join the dance, bright faces beam,
Sweet lips smile, and dark eyes gleam;
All these charms have hither come,
In honour of our Harvest Home.

Join the dance, with step as light,
As every heart should be to-night;
Music, shake the lofty dome,
In honour of our Harvest Home.

Quintet.

LUCY—ROSE—EDMUNDS—The SQUIRE—YOUNG BENSON.

No light bound
Of stag or timid hare,
O'er the ground
Where startled herds repair,
Do we prize
So high, or hold so dear,
As the eyes
That light our pleasures here.

No cool breeze
That gently plays by night,
O'er calm seas,
Whose waters glisten bright;
No soft moan
That sighs across the lea,
Harvest Home,
Is half so sweet as thee!

Chorus.

Hail to the merry autumn days, when yellow cornfields shine,
Far brighter than the costly cup that holds the monarch's wine!
Hail to the merry harvest time, the gayest of the year,
The time of rich and bounteous crops, rejoicing, and good cheer.

Charles Dickens - A Short Biography

Charles Dickens (1812-1870) is regarded by many readers and literary critics to be THE major English novelist of the Victorian Age. He is remembered today as the author of a series of weighty novels which have been translated into many languages and promoted to the rank of World Classics. The latter include, but are not limited to, *The Adventures of Oliver Twist*, *A Tale of Two Cities*, *David Copperfield*, *A Christmas Carol*, *Hard Times*, *Great Expectations* and *The Old Curiosity Shop*.

Birth and Childhood's Hardships

By and large, Charles Dickens's life story is one of somebody who is born and raised in dire straits to become one of the greatest men who have marked human history and thought. It is a perfect example of how the plight of the deprived and the destitute could transform into a precious incentive that pushes them to challenge their circumstances and to unexpectedly excel and shine.

Charles Dickens was born in Portsmouth on February 7th, 1812. His father John Dickens worked as a simple accounting clerk at the Naval Pay Office and the family's pecuniary situation was almost always uneven. When Charles was only two years, the family had to move to London, then later to Chatham. For financial reasons, Charles did not have adequate education. He rather had to leave school at a very young age to work at a polishing and blacking factory. To add insult to injury, Charles's father was imprisoned in 1824 after failing to pay a 40-pound debt.

Charles's experience at the factory played a tremendous role in building the novelist's personality and in deepening his concerns about working children and about the working class in general. Dickens's precocious maturity and the serious responsibilities that he had as a little child left a clear impression on many of his young characters, such as Oliver Twist, David Copperfield and Pip in *Great Expectations*. The hardships that Charles Dickens personally went through made him much interested in defending the poor, in fighting social injustice through exposing its blatant manifestations and in accentuating the importance of having decent work conditions.

Between 1824 and 1827, Dickens's father, who eventually managed to pay his debts, offered Charles the opportunity to attend a private school in North London, the Wellington House Academy. The experience surely enriched the young man's knowledge of the rules of writing and rhetoric and whetted his appetite for 18th-century novels and for the picaresque novels that adorned his father's library. However, during this period, Charles still had to experience another disappointment when his mother refused to spare him the strenuous job at the blacking factory even after the relative improvement of the family's financial situation. The mother's decision had a great psychological impact on young Charles and even influenced his vision of gender roles as he thought that the mother should not be the decision-maker in the family.

Early Publications

Young Charles Dickens occupied numerous jobs and worked hard to learn shorthand. This long and diversified professional experience had a patent impact on his different writings. Indeed, after the blacking factory experience, Dickens first worked as a clerk for attorneys, which allowed him to learn about the legal system and its principles, to become a free-lance reporter for Doctor's Commons Courts in 1829. Later, he even wrote reports for the House of Commons before starting to work for newspapers, magazines and journals.

It was in 1833 that Dickens started writing short stories for a number of literary magazines and journals such as *The Monthly Magazine.* A collection of these texts was later pseudonymously published under the title *Sketches by Boz*. Thanks to Dickens's humor and exceptional writing style, the latter publication was relatively successful, but not as successful as *The Pickwick Papers* whose serial publication sold thousands of copies and raised Dickens to considerable fame. In 1836, he started writing short texts to be published with the humorous illustrations of the famous artist Robert Seymour. These first successes encouraged Dickens to carry on publishing other stories in the form of series. Dickens's next creation was *Oliver Twist* which was published between 1837 and 1839.

It is noteworthy that most of Dickens's novels were published in the form of monthly and weekly chapters which, according to critics and biographers, allowed him to evaluate and adjust his characterizations and plots to meet the expectations of his readership. It was also during this period that Dickens started his long career as a literary magazine editor.

Loves and Marriage

Charles Dickens got married on April 2nd, 1836 to Catherine Thomson Hogarth after one year of engagement. They settled at the famous Furnival's Inn in Holborn, London, before they moved to their home in Bloomsbury. The house was transformed into the Charles Dickens Museum in 1925. Charles and Catherine, who lived there with the first three of their ten children, were joined by Charles's brother Frederick and Catherine's sister Mary. The latter was reported to have had a very special place in Charles's heart. After dying in his own arms in 1837 following a sudden illness, she became a source of inspiration for some of his female characters. After three years of marriage, Dickens's success and rising income made him leave the house for larger and more luxurious estates.

Catherine Hogarth was not Dickens's only love, however. Indeed, biographers report that Dickens's relation with his wife was sandwiched by two other romantic affairs. First, there was Maria Beadnell, a banker's daughter, with whom Dickens fell in love when he was only eighteen years old. The relationship ended three years later when Maria's parents apparently intervened. The other love story that Dickens went through started in 1857 and pushed him to divorce Catherine the following year. It was when Dickens was having a group of young actresses for the staging of his play *The Frozen Deep* that he fell in love with the actress Ellen Ternan who was 27 years younger than him.

Major Achievements

Charles's first success with *The Pickwick Papers* and *Oliver Twist* only pushed him to devote more time and energy to his writing and editorial activities. After publishing *Nicholas Nickleby* between 1838 and 1839, he started a new project in 1840 that he entitled *Master Humphrey's Clock*. The latter is a collection of stories that share the same frame and have recurring characters. It was among this collection that the two major works *The Old Curiosity Shop* and *Barnaby Rudge* were serially published.

After visiting the United States of America in 1842, Dickens developed a rather negative view of the New World which was mainly depicted in his travelogue *American Notes for General Circulation* and also in his picaresque novel *Martin Chuzzlewit*. The latter included very harsh satire of the republic and strongly denounced its institution of slavery. However, the fury that Dickens caused among some American circles was soon quietened with the publication of *A Christmas Carol* in 1843. The book, which is considered by many as the novelist's finest opus, was celebrated both in England and America.

Two other Christmas books followed respectively in 1834 and 1845. They are *The Chimes* and *The Cricket on the Hearth*. During this period,

Dickens also published a new travelogue that he entitled *Pictures from Italy* following his stay in the Mediterranean country. Another Christmas story entitled *The Haunted Man* was published in 1848, which was preceded by *Dombey and Son* (1847) and *The Battle of Life* (1847) and followed by David Copperfield (1849-1850), *Bleak House* (1852-1853) and *Hard Times* (1854).

It was in 1853 that Dickens started organizing public performances in which he presented his literary works. By this time, he also started to collaborate with Wilkie Collins on a number of short stories and plays. *Little Dorrit* started as a monthly serial in 1855 to be finished in 1857. Later, two of Dickens's most valuable works were published: *A Tale of Two Cities* (1859) and *Great Expectations* (1861). They were both published in the weekly periodical, *All the Year Round*, which he founded and edited himself.

Apart from his writings, Dickens's main profitable activity was the public reading of his novels. Along with the money he earned thanks to his successful publications, public readings allowed Dickens to buy his dream house (Gad's Hill Place, Kent), to offer financial help to his parents and brothers and to engage in charitable activities.

Twilight and Death

During the 1860s, Dickens carried on organizing more reading tours. In addition to the many events he had in England, he visited France, the United States, Scotland and Ireland on many an occasion. In 1864, he started his last complete novel, *Our Mutual Friend*. However, by 1865, his health started to waver. This was mainly because of the physical and intellectual exhaustion to which he subjected himself. Furthermore, Dickens was psychologically traumatized in 1865 following a train crash. He was with his beloved Ellen Ternan on their way back from Paris when their train derailed to cause a big number of casualties. Although Dickens was able to collect his courage and managed to help the wounded and comfort them, the picture of the disaster affected him greatly and could never be erased from his mind.

For health reasons, Dickens cancelled many of his programmed readings between 1868 and 1870. On April 22nd, 1869, he had a stroke. The latter was followed by a second stroke on June 8th, 1870, while he was working on his novel *The Mystery of Edwin Drood* which would remain unfinished. The next day, he passed away. Charles Dickens today rests in The Poets' Corner of Westminster Abbey.

www.ingramcontent.com/pod-product-compliance
Lightning Source LLC
Chambersburg PA
CBHW060059050426
42448CB00011B/2545